States of Matter in the Real World

by Roberta Baxter

Content Consultant
Dr. Tony Borgerding
Professor of Chemistry
University of St. Thomas

CORE
LIBRARY

Published by ABDO Publishing Company, PO Box 398166, Minneapolis, MN 55439. Copyright © 2013 by Abdo Consulting Group, Inc. International copyrights reserved in all countries. No part of this book may be reproduced in any form without written permission from the publisher. The Core Library™ is a trademark and logo of ABDO Publishing Company.

Printed in the United States of America,
North Mankato, Minnesota
112012
012013

♻ THIS BOOK CONTAINS AT LEAST 10% RECYCLED MATERIALS.

Editor: Karen Latchana Kenney
Series Designer: Becky Daum

Cataloging-in-Publication Data
Baxter, Roberta.
  States of matter in the real world / Roberta Baxter.
    p. cm. -- (Science in the real world)
Includes bibliographical references and index.
ISBN 978-1-61783-795-1
1. Matter--Juvenile literature. 2. Matter--Constitution--Juvenile literature. 3. Matter--Properties--Juvenile literature.   I. Title.
530.4--dc21

                                          2012946823

CONTENTS

CHAPTER ONE

What Are States of Matter?

The world around us is made of matter. Matter is made of tiny particles that we can't see, called atoms. They take up space and have mass. The chair you sit on, the air around you, your body, and even the stars are made of matter.

Matter comes in different forms. Water is an example. It is a liquid you drink or see in an ocean. But water also exists as solid ice and as gaseous steam

The stars of the Milky Way galaxy, as seen above Brazil, are made of matter.

from a teapot. Steam, liquid water, and ice are the states of matter of water.

All matter can exist in these three states. Some substances will be liquids at room temperature, while others will be solids or gases. It depends on the substance. The state of matter of any substance can be changed. A fourth state of matter, called plasma, can be found in stars and lightning.

Everyday Matter

The electricity in your home may come from a power plant that heats water until it turns to steam. The steam turns a big machine that produces the electricity. Air conditioners and refrigerators work by making liquid change to gas and back again.

Changing States

The state of matter of any substance can be changed. A solid changes to a liquid if heat is added. A liquid becomes a gas if heated. A gas changes to liquid when it cools. Liquids also change to solids in lower temperatures.

Water turns to gas when heated in a teapot.

CHAPTER TWO

Early Studies of Matter

Ancient Greek philosophers Democritus and Leucippus thought about the nature of matter. They guessed that it was possible to cut matter into its smallest pieces. They called those pieces *atomos* (or atoms). They also believed that atoms could not be destroyed. And they thought that atoms were combined in different ways to make all the things on Earth. Their idea of atoms was different from what

Greek philosopher Democritus thought about what matter was made from on Earth.

current scientists know about atoms. But the ancient Greeks had a great start to understanding matter.

Early Experiments

Early scientists knew of solids and liquids. They combined the two in different ways. Some noticed chemical reactions between the two that caused bubbles. Scientists later discovered that these bubbles were another form of matter—gas.

Scientist Robert Boyle investigated air. In 1660 he found that it could be compressed. His work resulted in Boyle's law. This law was about how the volume of gas related to pressure.

In 1756 Joseph Black found a gas that would not allow a candle to

Squeezed Air

Scientist Robert Boyle built a J-shaped glass tube. His assistant poured mercury, a heavy liquid, into the top of the tube. The mercury trapped a pocket of air in the short end. Boyle measured the air pocket. When more mercury was poured in, the pocket shrank. The air was squeezed together. This meant the air could be compressed.

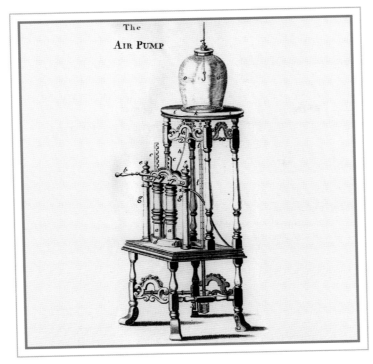

The
AIR PUMP

Robert Boyle used an air pump for his experiments with air and pressure.

burn. He called it "fixed air," but we now know it as carbon dioxide. Ten years later Henry Cavendish announced the discovery of the gas we call hydrogen. In 1774 Joseph Priestley produced a gas that would make a candle burn more brightly. He breathed in some of the gas. He said it made him breathe light and easy. He had discovered oxygen.

From 1772 to 1777, chemist Antoine Lavoisier discovered that air was made of more than one gas. Lavoisier also studied chemical reactions. He found that matter never disappears. It only changes form. This was the basis for the law of the conservation of mass. This theory states that in chemical reactions, mass is neither created nor destroyed.

Studying Atoms

In 1897 English scientist J. J. Thompson discovered the electron. People at the time knew that atoms were in all matter, but they did not know that atoms were made of smaller parts. Atoms are too small to see, so not much was known about them. Also around this time, scientist Marie Curie studied substances, such as uranium, that let off rays of energy. Ernest Rutherford showed that an atom's nucleus was small and dense in 1911. Then in 1913 Niels Bohr came up with the atomic model. This model showed that electrons moved in rings around the nucleus of an atom. He said that electrons could jump from one ring to another.

By learning more about atoms, these and other scientists discovered more about the nature of matter.

Author Jim Baggot wrote in his book *The Quantum Story* about important moments in the study of the atom. Baggot included a quote from Niels Bohr discussing his atomic model:

> "These models," [Bohr] had said, "have been deduced, or if you prefer, guessed, from experiments, not [proven math equations]. I hope that they describe the structure of atoms as well, but only as well, as is possible in the descriptive language of classical physics. We must be clear that, when it comes to atoms, language can be used only as in poetry. The poet, too, is not nearly so concerned with describing facts as with creating images and establishing mental connections."

Source: Jim Baggot. The Quantum Story: A History in 40 Moments. New York: Oxford University Press, 2011. Print. 47.

Consider Your Audience

Read this passage closely. How could you adapt Bohr's words for a modern audience, such as your neighbors or your classmates? Write a blog post giving this same information to the new audience. What is the most effective way to get your point across to this audience? How is the language you use for the new audience different from Bohr's original text? Why?

CHAPTER THREE

Solids Hold Their Shape

Much of the world is made up of solid materials. Wood, metal, and paper are all solids. We even use the word *solid* to mean something that is firm and strong.

What Is a Solid?

The atoms in matter have energy. They vibrate at different speeds. The amount of energy in matter determines if something is liquid, gas, or solid. Lots

Car frames are made from metal, which is a solid.

In solids, atoms are packed together but also have some space between them, similar to the balls in this picture.

of energy leads to a gas. Less energy leads to a solid state of matter.

Atoms are packed closely together in solids. Imagine some balls packed in a box. There is space between the balls, but not very much. Each ball touches several others. Like balls in a box, atoms in the solid state cannot be compressed.

Volume and Shape

Volume is how much space something takes up. If the same number of balls is put in a deeper box, the volume of the balls will stay the same. If you put salt in a test tube, it might take up half the tube. If it is spread out over the table, it looks different but still has the same volume. Atoms also keep the same volume. A solid will hold its shape unless a physical force acts on it. For example, a wad of clay will hold its shape unless someone starts squeezing it into a different shape.

Atoms in a solid state vibrate slowly because they have only a small amount of energy. They are attracted to one another so they stick together. When heat is added, the atoms vibrate faster. This can make a solid change its state. It can turn into a liquid.

Crystals

Many solids have a crystal structure. That means they have a regular, repeating pattern. Table salt and sugar may appear the same, but if you look at both

Studying Crystals

In the 1940s and 1950s, Dorothy Crowfoot Hodgkin studied crystals to figure out the three-dimensional structures of some really big molecules. She used X-rays on crystals to learn about the molecules' structures. Through her studies, Hodgkin discovered the structure of penicillin, an antibiotic, and insulin, a chemical that helps our bodies use sugar for energy. Hodgkin was awarded the 1964 Nobel Prize in Chemistry for her work.

under a microscope you will see a difference. The crystals of salt are cubic, like building blocks. Sugar crystals are longer and have six sides, like a hexagon. Another crystal is snow. Water droplets freeze into six-sided snowflakes with many different side branches and arms.

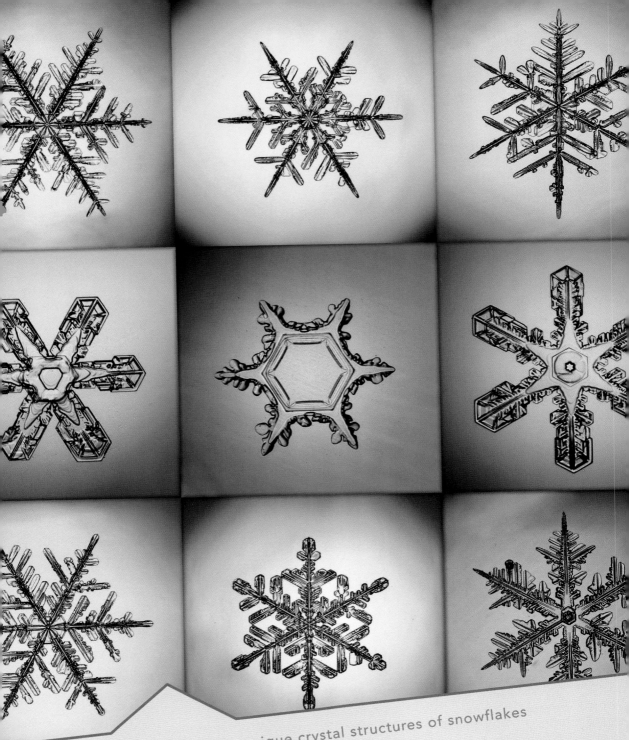

We can see the unique crystal structures of snowflakes when they are magnified.

CHAPTER FOUR

Flowing Liquids

Another state of matter is liquid. Water is the most common liquid found on Earth. Many liquids, such as milk, juice, and soft drinks, are mostly water. But other liquids include alcohols and gasoline.

Same Volume, Different Shapes

Atoms in liquids move past one another. They still pull toward each other, but they are not packed as tightly

Water is found in lakes, rivers, and oceans on Earth.

Liquids take on the shapes of their containers.

together as the atoms in solids. Most liquids, except for water, do not form crystals as solids do.

In one way liquids are like solids. They keep the same volume regardless of what container they are in. An amount of milk might look like more in a tall, skinny glass than in a short, fat one. But if the amounts were measured, they would be the same. The milk took on the shape of the glass but had the same volume.

Liquids are also very different from solids. Liquids take the shape of whatever container they are in.

They don't keep their shape as solids do. Instead they spread out to fill the container. Liquids can't be compressed or squeezed closer together. The atoms are already close to one another.

Atoms in liquids have more energy than those in solids and less than those in gases. Atoms in liquids slide past other atoms. This makes liquids flow. Liquids change state when heated or cooled. Adding heat turns a liquid into a gas. Cooling a liquid changes it into a solid.

Surface Tension

One way liquids are different from the other states of matter is that they have surface tension. Think of water hitting a newly waxed car. The water forms beads on the car rather than flowing

Water Is Different

Most solids are denser than the liquid state of the same substance. The solid will sink to the bottom of a container holding the liquid. Water is different. Ice is the solid form of water. And ice is less dense than liquid water. Ice does not sink. It floats. This is important to fish in a lake. During winter some of the water freezes above and protects the fish below.

over it. This happens because of surface tension. The molecules of water are more strongly attached to one another than they are to the wax on the car. This causes beads to form. Surface tension also allows some insects, such as a water strider, to walk on water.

FURTHER EVIDENCE

There was quite a bit of information about liquids in Chapter Four. It covered the properties of liquids, including surface tension. But if you could pick out the main point of the chapter, what would it be? What evidence was given to support that point? Visit the Web site below to learn more about surface tension and water. Choose a quote from the Web site that relates to this chapter. Does this quote support the author's main point? Does it make a new point? Write a few sentences explaining how the quote you found relates to this chapter.

What Is Surface Tension?

www.epa.gov/owow/NPS/kids/surfacetension.html

Water striders use surface tension to walk on water.

CHAPTER FIVE

Moving Gases

The third common state of matter is gas. Air is a mixture of gases. The reaction when baking soda and vinegar are mixed results in a bubbling gas. This is carbon dioxide. You can also see this gas as bubbles in a soft drink or sparkling water.

Volume and Shape

Gases take the shape of whatever container they are placed in. They have no shape of their own.

The bubbles in sparkling water are caused by a gas in the water.

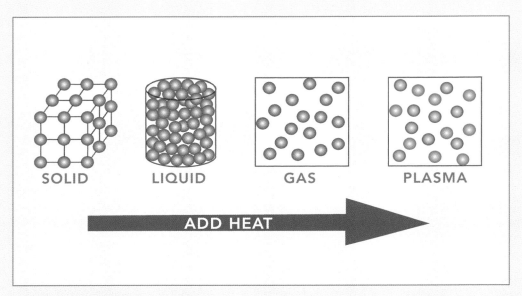

Moving Atoms

The atoms in different states of matter move at different speeds. They also have more or less space between them. Take a look at this diagram. Compare how the information is conveyed visually in the diagram with how it's conveyed in the text. How are they similar? How are they different?

If an amount of gas in a small container is let into a larger container, the gas will fill up the larger container.

In solids and liquids, atoms are strongly attracted to one another. But in gases, there is only a weak attraction. Each gas atom bounces in every direction. It does not slow down and stop. This state of matter has much more energy than either liquids or solids.

Gases fill up and take the shape of hot air balloons.

Gases exert pressure. The pressure comes from the gas atoms hitting the sides of the container. Gases can be compressed into smaller places. If a force is applied to compress the gas, the atoms squeeze together. For example air inside a partly filled balloon can be compressed into a tight section of the balloon.

Compressed Gas

A bottle of liquid oxygen can hold a large amount of gaseous oxygen. The bottle of gaseous oxygen can be easily strapped to a person's back or rolled on a little cart. Compression makes it easy to carry around a large amount of a gas in a small container.

Changing State

When a gas cools, the atoms slow down. They stick to each other. They turn into a liquid. The ability to compress gases by squeezing them with pressure is very useful. Scuba divers and people needing oxygen because of health problems use tanks of compressed oxygen. Inside the tanks the oxygen is a liquid. It expands when it is released. It turns back into a gas to be breathed. Another property of gas is its ability to diffuse. Perfumes and even the scent of a skunk turn quickly from a liquid into a gas. Then the gas mixes with the air, spreading the smell.

Antoine Lavoisier studied gases in the 1700s. He wrote about the nature of gases in *Memoir on the Combustion in General*:

> *All bodies in nature present themselves to us in three different states. Some are solid like stones, earth, salt, and metals. Others are fluid like water, mercury, spirits of wine; and others finally are in a third state which I shall call the state of expansion or of vapours. . . The same body can pass successfully through each of these states, and in order to make this phenomenon occur it is necessary only to combine it with a greater or lesser quantity of the matter of fire.*

Source: William H. Brock. The Norton History of Chemistry. New York: W. W. Norton & Co., 1992. Print. 98.

What's the Big Idea?

Take a close look at Lavoisier's words. What is his main idea? What evidence does he use to support this idea? Come up with a few sentences showing how Lavoisier uses two or three pieces of evidence to support his main point.

CHAPTER SIX

Changing States of Matter

Changing from one state to another involves energy, usually in the form of heat. The heat can be added or removed.

For a solid to melt into a liquid, the attractions between its atoms must be weakened. When heat is added, atoms gain enough energy to partially overcome the attractions rigidly holding them

Metal turns to liquid if it is heated to a high temperature.

together in a solid. The solid becomes a liquid by melting.

The same happens when a liquid turns into a gas. The atoms gain energy from heat and completely overcome the attractions holding them together. The atoms begin moving around very fast and in a random manner. This makes the liquid turn into a gas. This process is called vaporization. When a liquid boils and evaporates, it is part of this process.

Taking Away Heat

When heat is taken away, the states of matter also change. Cooling a gas will turn it into a liquid. This process is called condensation. A liquid freezes into a solid when heat is taken away. Compression can also turn gases into liquids.

Dry ice turns from solid to gas without a liquid state in between.

Some substances can change from a solid to a gas without the liquid stage. This is called sublimation. Sometimes snow will disappear when the solid crystal turns into water vapor. Solid carbon dioxide, or dry ice, also turns from a solid to a gas.

Deposition is the opposite of sublimation. Deposition is occurring when frost builds up on a window.

Identifying Substances

Melting temperature and boiling point can be used to identify unknown substances. A melting temperature is the point at which a solid substance melts. The

Chemical name	Melting point	Boiling point
Gold	1945.4°F (1063°C)	
Yellow brass	1661°F to 1709.6°F (905°C to 932°C)	
Methanol (Wood Alcohol)		148.93°F (64.96°C)
Isopropanol (Rubbing Alcohol)		180.5°F (82.5°C)
Water	32°F (0°C)	212°F (100°C)

Melting and Boiling Points

Here are some melting and boiling points that can be used to identify chemicals. Take a look at this chart. What do these temperatures tell you about the chemicals in the table? How might a scientist use this information?

boiling point of a liquid is the temperature at which it turns into a gas. Suppose you had two gold-colored pieces of metal and you needed to find out which one is gold. If you melted one and it turned into a liquid at 1945.4 degrees Fahrenheit (1063°C), then that piece is gold. If the piece melted at a lower temperature, then it is not gold. It is yellow brass. Two types of chemicals called alcohols are both clear liquids. But their boiling temperatures are different. This identifies the liquids.

A metal worker melts gold at a very high and specific temperature.

CHAPTER SEVEN

Plasma In the Stars

Another state of matter is seen in the stars. It is called plasma. Because plasma exists in the stars, it is the most common state of matter in the universe. This state of matter has a changing volume and shape. In gases the atoms zoom around with their electrons intact. But in plasma the electrons are stripped away from the atom by an enormous amount of energy.

A green aurora borealis display, made from plasma particles reacting with Earth's atmosphere, glows over a city in Norway.

Sir William Crookes described the plasma state of matter in 1879. American chemist Dr. Irving Langmuir gave plasma its name in 1923. A gas can become plasma when heated to extremely high temperatures, such as those found in our sun and other stars. The sun releases plasma plumes from its surface. These plasma particles travel to Earth. This flow is called the solar wind. When it reaches Earth, the energy of the plasma hits gas atoms in the atmosphere and causes them to glow. The result is the aurora borealis (the northern lights) or the aurora australis (the southern lights). Plasma also occurs in lightning.

On Earth scientists have learned to make the plasma state and to control it. Some televisions and all fluorescent lights contain plasma. The plasma they contain is created from electric currents sent through gas.

The states of matter are an important part of our world. Everything we see and touch is a solid, liquid, gas, or plasma. The next time you feel a popsicle melting in your mouth, see a lightning bolt, or touch a table, you will be experiencing the different states of matter.

EXPLORE ONLINE

The focus in Chapter Seven was plasma. It also touched upon where plasma is found. The Web site below focuses on the same subjects. As you know, every source is different. How is the information given in the Web site different from the information in this chapter? What information is the same? How do the two sources present information differently? What can you learn from this Web site?

Plasma Basics
www.chem4kids.com/files/matter_plasma.html

IMPORTANT DATES

1660
Robert Boyle shows that air can be compressed.

1756
Joseph Black discovers carbon dioxide.

1766
Henry Cavendish discovers hydrogen.

1774
Joseph Priestley discovers oxygen.

1879
Sir William Crookes discovers plasma.

1897
J. J. Thompson discovers the electron.

1911
Ernest Rutherford describes an atom's nucleus as small and dense.

1913
Niels Bohr creates an atomic model.

1923
Irving Langmuir names the new state of matter plasma.

1940s–1950s
Dorothy Crowfoot Hodgkin studies crystals to understand the structure of large molecules.

OTHER WAYS YOU CAN FIND STATES OF MATTER IN THE REAL WORLD

Helium Balloons

Helium balloons float high in the sky. Helium is a gas that is less dense than air. Since helium is lighter, it floats in air. But a helium balloon in the air will soon be down on the ground. Why? Helium is a very small atom, and it leaks out of the balloon. It diffuses through the wall of the balloon, so the balloon does not float anymore.

What Is the Dew Point?

The dew point is a measure of how much water vapor is in the air. You might hear the dew point mentioned on a weather forecast. If the temperature cools to the dew point, the water vapor condenses out of the air and becomes dew or fog. The dew point is always lower than or equal to the air temperature.

Melting Ice

In winter you might spread solid salt on an icy sidewalk. The salt makes the ice melt, turning that solid into a liquid. One solid changes the state of another solid.

Say What?

Studying about the states of matter can mean learning a lot of new vocabulary. Find five words in this book you've never seen or heard before. Use a dictionary to find out what they mean. Then write the meanings in your own words, and use each word in a new sentence.

Another View

There are many sources online and in your library about the states of matter. Ask a librarian or other adult to help you find a reliable source on states of matter. Compare what you learn in this new source and what you have found out in this book. Then write a short essay comparing and contrasting the new source's view of states of matter to the ideas in this book. How are they different? How are they similar? Why do you think they are different or similar?

You Are There

Imagine that you are in Antoine Lavoisier's laboratory trying to discover what gases are in air. How would you measure the different gases, and what equipment would you need? What would your results be? What challenges would you have in doing the research?

Surprise Me

Learning about states of matter can be interesting and surprising. What two or three facts about states of matter did you find most surprising? Write a few sentences about each fact. Why did you find them surprising?

GLOSSARY

atoms
tiny particles that make
up matter

compressed
squeezed together

condensation
turning a gas into a liquid

crystal
a solid with a regular
repeating pattern

dense
heavy

deposition
the action of matter being
deposited in a layer on
something

diffuse
spread out

energy
the ability to do work

molecule
combination of atoms
bound together

sublimation
going from a solid directly
to a gas

vaporization
changing into a vapor or gas

volume
the amount of space
taken up by matter

LEARN MORE

Books

Brent, Lynnette. *States of Matter.* New York: Crabtree Publishing Company, 2008.

Johnson, Rebecca L. *Atomic Structure.* Minneapolis, MN: Twenty-First Century Books, 2008.

Peppas, Lynn. *What Is a Gas?* New York: Crabtree Publishing Company, 2013.

Web Links

To learn more about states of matter, visit ABDO Publishing Company online at **www.abdopublishing.com**. Web sites about states of matter are featured on our Book Links page. These links are routinely monitored and updated to provide the most current information available. Visit **www.mycorelibrary.com** for free additional tools for teachers and students.

How is science at work around us? Why is electricity important in daily life? Have you thought about how magnets are used in machines? And how do forces and motion affect transportation? Each book in the Science in the Real World series explores a different science concept, uncovering fascinating ways the concept is at work in everyday situations and technology.

CORE LIBRARY

Core Library is the must-have line of nonfiction books for supporting the Common Core State Standards for grades 3–6.

Core Library features:

- A wide variety of high-interest topics

- Well-researched, clearly written informational text

- Primary sources with accompanying questions

- Multiple prompts and activities for writing, reading, and critical thinking

- Charts, graphs, diagrams, timelines, and maps

Visit **www.mycorelibrary.com** for fre___ additional tools for teachers and stu___

Books in this set:
Electricity in the Real World
Energy in the Real World
Forces and Motion in the Real World
Light in the Real World
Magnets in the Real World
The Scientific Method in the Real World
Sound in the Real World
States of Matter in the Real World

ABDO
Publishing Company

ISBN: 978-1___

9 781617 837951

Forces and
Motion in the
Real World

by Kathleen M. Muldoon

Published by ABDO Publishing Company, PO Box 398166, Minneapolis, MN 55439. Copyright © 2013 by Abdo Consulting Group, Inc. International copyrights reserved in all countries. No part of this book may be reproduced in any form without written permission from the publisher. The Core Library™ is a trademark and logo of ABDO Publishing Company.

Printed in the United States of America,
North Mankato, Minnesota
112012
012013

Editor: Karen Latchana Kenney
Series Designer: Becky Daum

Cataloging-in-Publication Data
Muldoon, Kathleen M.
 Forces and motion in the real world / Kathleen M. Muldoon.
   p. cm. -- (Science in the real world)
Includes bibliographical references and index.
ISBN 978-1-61783-790-6
1. Force and energy--Juvenile literature.   I. Title.
531--dc21
                                                    2012946819

Photo Credits: Emilia Ungur/Shutterstock Images, cover, 1; Jamie McDonald/Getty Images, 4; Stock Montage/Getty Images, 8; Prisma/UIG/Getty Images, 10; General Photographic Agency/Getty Images, 12; Justin Sullivan/Getty Images, 14; Lars Baron/Bongarts/Getty Images, 16; Encyclopaedia Britannica/UIG/Getty Images, 18; Shutterstock Images, 20, 26; Chris Rutter/N-Photo Magazine/Getty Images, 23; Oleksii Sagitov/Shutterstock Images, 24; Stephen Mcsweeny/Shutterstock Images, 28; Red Line Editorial, 29, 40; Tom Wang/Shutterstock, 31, 45; NASA/Getty Images, 33; Shaun Botterill/Getty Images, 34; iStockphoto, 37, 38

CONTENTS

CHAPTER ONE

Push, Pull, and Move

When you kick a ball on a field, you know it will move forward. On your skateboard, you know going down a hill will make you speed up. And while gazing at the stars and moon, you are certain they will not suddenly fall from the sky. You know all these things are true. But you might not know *why* they are true.

Forces and motion are at work as a skateboarder gets air during a trick.

The Hubble Space Telescope

On April 24, 1990, the space shuttle *Discovery* launched a giant telescope into space. The Hubble space telescope is as big as a school bus. It is powered by light from the sun and is controlled by computers. Forces and motion keep the Hubble space telescope in orbit. It sends images to Earth that increase our knowledge of the universe. One image sent in 2011 showed a fifth moon orbiting Pluto.

Physics helps explain what we know or would like to know about how the world and universe works. Scientists have discovered natural laws that rule everything on our planet and the solar system. Some of these natural laws are about forces and motion. Forces are pushes or pulls that can make objects move or stop moving and can change the shape of an object. Motion is any movement or change in position. Without forces and motion, the world could not exist as we know it.

While holding a book, you may think you are sitting perfectly still. But there is motion within and around you. Invisible forces are at work keeping you alive. Your heart pumps blood to every cell in your body. Gravity pulls you toward Earth's center. Outside, birds fly, motors hum, and the whole world is in motion.

FURTHER EVIDENCE

Chapter One contains quite a bit of information about the study of forces and motion. It covers important scientists who have studied forces and motion. But if you could pick out the main point of the chapter, what would it be? What evidence was given to support that point? Visit the Web site below to learn more about forces and motion in everyday life. Choose a quote from the Web site that relates to this chapter. Does this quote support the author's main point? Does it make a new point? Write a few sentences explaining how the quote you found relates to this chapter.

Idaho Public Television: Gravity Facts
www.idahoptv.org/dialogue4kids/season12/gravity/facts.cfm

CHAPTER TWO

Studying Forces and Motion

Scientists have been studying forces and motion for centuries. Aristotle was an ancient Greek philosopher and scientist who lived from 384 to 322 BCE. He noticed that four elements made up the world: solids, liquids, gas, and fire. He believed that forces and motion happened when these elements tried to find their place in the world. Scientists later

Philosopher and scientist Aristotle, left, taught his studies to others, such as Alexander the Great, right.

Galileo Galilei studied the stars and thought about the forces on Earth and in space.

used some of his observations to understand forces and motion.

In 250 BCE Greek scientist Archimedes discovered the reason why some objects float and others sink. It depended on the volume of the object and the force of air or water on it. This theory proved to be true. Today engineers rely on Archimedes's discovery. It helps them design ships that float in water and planes that soar in air.

Modern Physics

Galileo Galilei has been called the father of modern physics. In 1609 CE he developed a telescope. Later in his career, Galileo tried to show that force and motion work together. In one experiment he dropped balls of different

A New Idea of Motion

Galileo learned about Aristotle's teachings on motion while in college at the University of Pisa. He did not agree with them though. His experiment dropping balls proved that Aristotle was wrong. Aristotle believed the heavier ball should have hit the ground first.

Albert Einstein studied gravity and forces.

weights from a tower. The balls hit the ground at the same time. This showed that objects fall at the same rate even if they are of different weights.

Sir Isaac Newton also discovered laws that run our universe. He added to work that Galileo had done. In 1687 Newton used math to create laws of motion. Scientists still use those laws today. Trains, cars, and spacecraft are designed based on Newton's laws of motion.

Albert Einstein was always interested in laws of nature. In 1907 he released his studies on the laws of gravity. This is the force that pulls you down to Earth.

Perhaps one of the most well-known physicists is Stephen Hawking. He has

Black Holes

The force of gravity causes black holes. Gravity's force is very strong in certain spots in outer space. A dying star can cause this strong force. It pulls so much that light cannot escape. You cannot see a black hole. But you can see the stars around one.

Physicist Stephen Hawking speaks about physics at the University of California, Berkeley, in 2007.

combined some of his theories with Einstein's. One of the many things he studies is how forces create black holes in space. His book *A Brief History of Time* was published on September 1, 1998. It helps us understand the effects of forces and motion in the universe.

In 1752 William Stukeley wrote a book about his friend Sir Isaac Newton's life. In it Stukeley wrote of a conversation he had with Newton:

> *After dinner, the weather being warm, we went into the garden and drank tea, under the shade of some apple trees . . . when formerly the notion of [gravity] came into his mind. "Why should that apple always [fall straight down] to the ground," thought he to himself, occasion'd by the fall of an apple, as he sat in a [thoughtful] mood. "Why should it not go sideways or upwards, but constantly to the earth's centre?"*
>
> Source: William Stukeley. *"Memoirs of Sir Isaac Newton's life."* Turning the Pages. *The Royal Society, n.d. Web. Accessed November 6, 2012.*

Consider Your Audience

Read Newton's quote from the passage above closely. How could you adapt Newton's words for a modern audience, such as your neighbors or your classmates? Write a blog post discussing the same observations and questions to the new audience. What is the most effective way to get your point across to this audience? How is language you use for the new audience different from Newton's quote? Why?

CHAPTER THREE

Forces Rule!

Forces rule our universe, our world, and us. We cannot actually see most forces, but we can feel their pushes and pulls.

There are four main types of forces: strong, electromagnetic, weak, and gravitational. Forces relate to atoms. An atom is the smallest part of all matter. It contains a nucleus made of protons

Wind is a force that cannot be seen, but its effects can be observed.

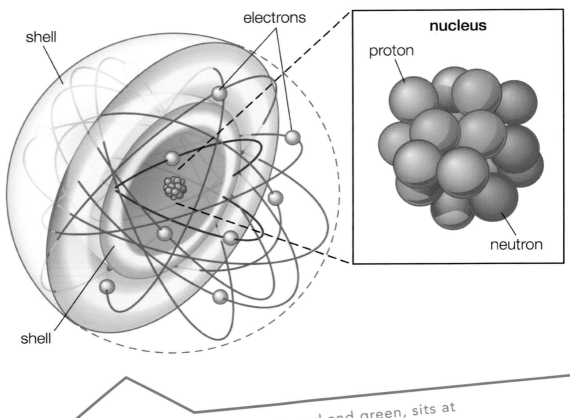

An atom's nucleus, shown in red and green, sits at its center.

and neutrons. Electrons float in shells around an atom's nucleus.

Strong and Weak Forces

The strong force is the force that keeps the nucleus together. It is very strong inside the nucleus, but cannot be felt far away from the nucleus. The weak force is the force that causes decay of small particles. Decay is when an atom's nucleus emits particles.

Electromagnetic Force

Electromagnetic force is seen in the electrical charge in parts of atoms. Electrons have a negative charge. Protons have a positive charge. Protons are attracted to electrons. This holds an atom's nucleus to its orbiting electrons. This force can be felt over long distances.

Friction is an electromagnetic force. Have you walked on carpet and then touched metal? The shock you received is caused by static electricity.

Magnetic Resonance Imaging

When doctors search for the cause of a person's illness, they may use magnetic resonance imaging (MRI). MRI machines are giant magnetic tubes. The patient slides into the machine on a flat table. After the machine is turned on, it creates a magnetic field. Atoms inside the patient reflect radio signals back to the MRI machine. A computer changes these signals into images of the patient's body.

Gravity holds the moon in Earth's orbit.

As you walk, your shoes rub on the carpet. This causes friction. The friction lifts electrons away from the carpet. Your body is now supercharged! If you touch metal and are in a dark room, you might see a tiny electrical spark jump from your fingers to the metal. This is static electricity, an electromagnetic force.

Gravitational Force

Gravity is an attracting force between two objects anywhere in the universe. On Earth gravity pulls everything toward its center. Gravity holds the moon, you, and everything else on Earth in place. You can't feel gravity, but it is always working upon you. Because our planet has more mass than the moon, Earth's gravity is stronger than gravity on the moon. Jupiter's gravity keeps at least 61 moons orbiting around it. Not even Galileo or Newton understood the exact cause of gravity's pulling force. But without it, everything in the universe would swirl about and smash into each other.

The Nature of Forces

Forces rarely work alone. Several forces may act on an object at the same time. For example, Earth's gravity holds ocean water to its surface, but gravity from the sun and moon pull oceans toward them. These different forces result in tides that change the position of the water.

Using Gravity to Map Mass

On March 17, 2002, NASA and the German Aerospace Center launched two satellites that use gravity to discover changes in Earth's mass. They are called the Gravity Recovery and Climate Experiment (GRACE) satellites. The information these satellites collect helps scientists find out the rate at which polar ice melts. Scientists find out the rate that polar ice melts in order to measure the changes in Earth's temperature. This information is especially useful for understanding global warming.

Balanced and Unbalanced

Forces don't always make objects move. Suppose a heavy book is placed on a table. The book's weight pushes it down on the table. The surface of the table pushes back on the book with equal force. Since the forces of the book's weight and the surface of the table are equal, they are in balance.

Balanced forces are two or more forces acting on an object at the same time. They do not change an object's motion because the forces are equal in strength.

Ocean tides are pulled and pushed by the gravity of Earth, the sun, and the moon.

Construction cranes use balanced forces to lift heavy objects.

Unbalanced forces are forces that cause a change in an object's position or motion. This is because one force is greater than another.

Stephen Hawking wrote about gravity in his book *A Briefer History of Time*. He said:

> *Gravity is the weakest of the four forces by a long way; it is so weak that we would not notice it at all were it not for two special properties that it has: it can act over long distances, and it is always attractive. This means that the very weak gravitational forces between the individual particles in two large bodies, such as the earth and the sun, can add up to produce a [very big] force.*

Source: Stephen Hawking and Leonard Mlodinow. A Briefer History of Time. New York: Bantam, 2005. Print. 120.

What's the Big Idea?

Take a close look at Hawking's words. What is his main idea? What evidence is used to support his point? Come up with a few sentences showing how Hawking uses two or three pieces of evidence to support his main point.

CHAPTER FOUR

Laws of Motion

Motion is about moving. Force gets objects moving. But motion is also about *how* things continue to move after that first force. Sir Isaac Newton discovered three laws that help us understand motion.

The First Law of Motion

This law has two parts. First an object at rest will stay at rest until an unbalanced force is put on it. For

The force of a push starts the motion of a swing.

A baseball changes direction when it is hit by a batter's bat.

example, if you toss your dirty socks on the bed, they will remain there until you push them off. Second, an object in motion will move in a straight line at a constant speed until an unbalanced force acts on it. When a batter hits a line drive, the ball continues

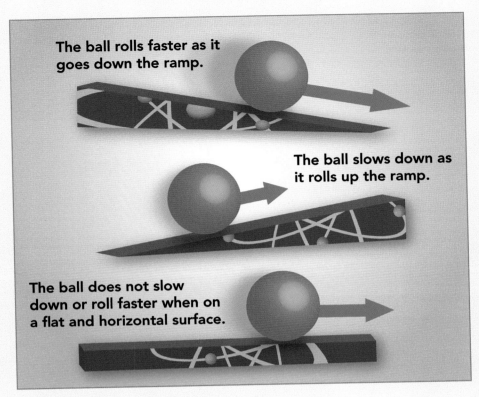

The ball rolls faster as it goes down the ramp.

The ball slows down as it rolls up the ramp.

The ball does not slow down or roll faster when on a flat and horizontal surface.

Newton's Laws in Action
This diagram shows how Newton's three laws of motion work upon a ball. The force pushed against the ball is a person's finger. After reading about Newton's laws, what does this diagram tell you? Does it help you better understand how the laws work?

moving forward until it is caught, hits a wall, or meets a force that changes its motion. Objects at rest or in motion in the same direction and at the same speed are in the state of inertia.

The Second Law of Motion

Acceleration is any increase in speed or change in direction caused by unbalanced forces. When force pushes on an object, it makes the object move in a certain direction. If the force acts in the direction of motion it will make the object have a greater speed. If the force acts opposite to the direction of motion it will make the object have a slower speed. A stronger force will change the motion faster than a weaker force.

The Motion of Earth's Plates

Massive sheets of solid rock, called plates, are always moving very slowly below Earth's surface. Earthquakes happen when one plate slips past or under another. Scientists use computers to follow the movement of Earth's plates. They combine that information with a measurement of the force of the surface above the plates. This force pushes against the plates. Knowing the force and movement allows scientists to better predict where earthquakes might occur.

The Third Law of Motion

This law tells us that for every action, there

Wind pushes back as a car speeds forward.

is an equal and opposite reaction. You can feel this law when you ride in a car. As it speeds forward, air pushes back against the car. The car's forward action is a push into the air, which causes the reaction of wind pushing back at the car.

Motion in Action

Motion affects our everyday lives and our universe. Whether we travel on foot, on a bike, in a car, or through the air, we like to know how fast we will get from here to there. The motion of objects moving in a line is an object's velocity.

Suppose, though, that rather than moving in a straight line, you are a figure skater spinning on a spot in the center of the ice. You are thinking more about staying upright than you are thinking about your speed. Centripetal force causes some objects to move in circles. A satellite orbits Earth because gravity pulls the satellite toward Earth's center.

A research satellite orbits Earth in 1991.

CHAPTER FIVE

Motion and Energy

In 1807 English scientist Thomas Young was the first person to study how objects in motion can be made to do work. He believed that the ability of an object to do work was its energy. Forces and motion play an important role in an object's energy. Scientists have found many types of energy. Two major types are kinetic energy and potential energy.

The force of a foot on a soccer ball is changed into the kinetic energy of the ball.

Kinetic and Potential Energy

Any moving object able to do work has kinetic energy. This is the energy of motion. Moving objects can change from one form of energy to another. For example, whirling blades on windmills convert the wind's kinetic energy into electric energy.

Scientists have also discovered that energy can be stored for later use. Potential energy is one example of stored energy. It is due to an object's position. Imagine an enormous wrecking ball dangling from a cable on a crane. The raised ball has potential energy. Then the crane operator puts the cable in motion and swings the ball into the wall of a building. It crashes through a wall, pushing it inside the

Kinetic Energy and Sports

Because kinetic energy is the energy of motion, many sports involve athletes transferring kinetic energy to sports objects. Rolled bowling balls and hit racquetballs have kinetic energy. Some athletes have kinetic energy in their bodies, such as runners racing along a track.

A wrecking ball has potential energy.

building. The potential energy of the wrecking ball now becomes kinetic energy.

Getting and Storing Energy

Scientists and engineers have experimented with ways of getting and storing energy. Many of these ways of storing energy are very useful.

Solar cells can provide energy to a home.

Magnets use the natural force of magnetism. They are used in everything from computer discs to motors. Electrical lines carry electricity away from power stations where it is made. These lines bring electricity to your home. Batteries make and store chemical energy. Nuclear energy is produced in reactors. Atoms are split apart inside the reactors. This releases energy that is used for electricity. The energy is then stored in another part of the nuclear power plant until it is needed. Much of the power for homes and businesses in the United States is supplied by nuclear energy.

Clean Energy

Scientists have also found a way to capture energy from the sun. This is called solar power. Horace Bénédict de Saussure built the first solar power collector in 1767. Solar panels capture energy from the sun. This energy is stored in the panels' cells. Solar panels can be mounted on roofs of houses.

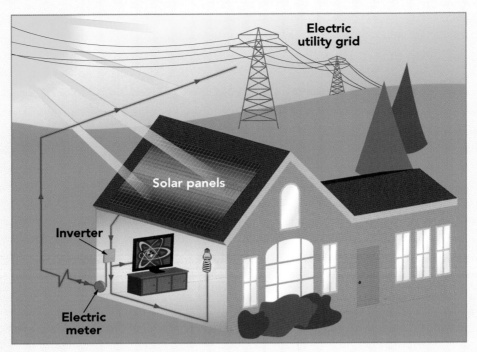

Harnessing Energy from the Sun

This diagram shows how solar panels take power from the sun and store it for use as energy in homes. Excess energy can flow back into the utility grid from the house. After reading about solar panels in this chapter, how did you think they sent power to a home? How has that idea changed after looking at this diagram? How does seeing this diagram help you better understand how solar power works?

Another source of clean energy is the wind. Wind is air in motion. Engineers have designed machines that use blades to capture the wind's kinetic energy. The blades are connected to motors that create electricity. In 2011 wind turbines produced 3 percent of the electricity generated in the United States.

Moving water can also provide usable energy. Scientists and engineers have developed machines to collect the energy in rivers, streams, and oceans. One of these machines is called a wave energy converter. It collects water, which is then run through an engine that stores the energy.

Try to imagine your life in a world and universe not ruled by the laws of forces and motion. Could such a place exist? Could you exist? Forces and motion rule how we move and work every day.

IMPORTANT DATES

300s BCE
Aristotle notices four elements make up the world and believes they cause motion.

250 BCE
Archimedes discovers why some objects float or sink.

1600s CE
Galileo Galilei experiments with gravity using balls.

1687
Sir Isaac Newton writes about the laws of motion.

1767
Physicist Horace Bénédict de Saussure builds the first solar power collector.

1807
Thomas Young studies how objects in motion can be made to do work.

1907
Albert Einstein releases studies on the laws of gravity.

1990
On April 24 the Hubble space telescope is launched into space.

1998
Stephen Hawking's book *A Brief History of Time* is released on September 1.

2002
Gravity Recovery and Climate Experiment (GRACE) satellites are launched on March 17.

2011
A Hubble space telescope image shows a fifth moon orbiting Pluto.

OTHER WAYS YOU CAN FIND FORCES AND MOTION IN THE REAL WORLD

Beetles with Backpacks

Scientists at the University of Michigan have found a way to get energy from the movement of beetles. This kinetic energy then powers tiny cameras and sensors in a pack strapped to the backs of the insects. The beetles, called "cyborgs," can be sent into dangerous places such as buildings where there has been a chemical spill. The equipment in the beetles' backpacks record information that will let firefighters and other rescuers know if it is safe for them to enter.

Solar-Powered House Paint

Imagine being able to have solar power in a home by just applying a coat of fresh paint. Researchers at the University of Notre Dame have developed paint that they named "Sun-Believable." It has tiny particles that are able to capture solar power to make energy. Scientists are hoping to make the paint better over time so that it will capture even more solar power.

Amazing Hovercraft

Hovercrafts are truly all-terrain vehicles. They can travel over land or water. They come in all shapes and sizes, but they have the same three basic parts: a flat surface or platform, a motorized fan, and a skirt. The skirt is on the bottom of the hovercraft and allows it to get over things. Hovercrafts move because the air flowing through chambers in the skirt creates air pressure that is higher than the air pressure outside. This creates an air cushion on which hovercraft ride. They skim approximately 9 inches (23 cm) above surfaces, reducing the friction and making a smooth ride.

Say What?

Studying forces and motion can mean learning a lot of new vocabulary. Find five words in this book that you've never heard before. Use a dictionary to find out what they mean. Then write the meanings in your own words, and use each word in a new sentence.

Dig Deeper

What questions do you still have about Newton's laws of motion? Do you want to learn more about how they cause moving objects to behave? Or do you want to study more examples of these laws in action? Write down one or two questions that can guide you in doing your research. With an adult's help, find a few reliable new sources about Newton's laws of motion that can help answer your questions. Write a few sentences about how you did your research and what you learned from it.

Why Do I Care?

This book explains how forces and motion affect your life every day. List two or three ways that you use forces and motion in your life. For example, what forces do you feel when you ride a bike?

Tell the Tale

This book discusses the laws of forces and motion, which lead to energy. These laws were not recently discovered. In about 200 words, write the story of the history leading to our understanding of forces and motion. Be sure to set the scene, include several different events, and have a conclusion.

GLOSSARY

acceleration
any increase in speed or change in direction caused by unbalanced forces

electromagnetic
the force that holds atoms together

energy
the ability to produce work

forces
pushes or pulls that can make objects move or stop moving and can change the shape of an object

friction
a force that resists or starts the motion of an object

gravity
a force that attracts all objects to all other objects

inertia
state of objects at rest or in motion in the same direction and at the same speed

mass
a measure of the tendency of an object to resist a change in motion

motion
any change in position; movement

theory
a view of the behavior of our physical world which is testable by experiment and observation

velocity
the speed of an object moving in one direction